IN FOCUS: NATIVE AMERICANS

CHOCTAW

HISTORY AND CULTURE

MARK STEWART

Cavendish Square

Published in 2026 by Cavendish Square Publishing, LLC
2544 Clinton Street, Buffalo, NY 14224

Website: cavendishsq.com

Portions of this work were originally authored by Ada Quinlivan and published as *Choctaw* (Spotlight on Native Americans). All new material this edition authored by Mark Stewart.

Publisher: Katie Kawa
Book Design: Lisa Miley

Portions of this work were reviewed by: Donald A. Grinde, Jr., Professor of Transnational/American Studies at the State University of New York at Buffalo.

Photo Credits: Jody Dingle/Shutterstock.com (4); Bernard Romans (5*); MPI/Archive Photos/Getty Images (6, 10, 18); George Catlin/National Gallery of Art (7*, 10*, 16*, 23*); Project Gutenberg (9*); H. Charles McBarron/U.S. Army Center of Military History (11*); Sotheby's (12); McKenney and Hall (13*); Author's Collection (14); Alfred Boisseau (17*); M.R. Harrington/Smithsonian Institution (19 top*); Choctaw Nation of Oklahoma (19 bottom*); Ditch Fisher/Wikimedia Commons (20); Patina Picker (21); Courtesy of LeAnne Howe (22); U.S. Department of the Interior (23); Smithsonian Institution (25*); Niall Carson/PA Images via Getty Images (26); Jen Band of Choctaw Indians (27); Kevin Jackson, AMC/US Army (28); Carlisle Indian School Digital Resource Center (29). *These images are in the public domain.

Cover images (clockwise from top): MPI/Archive Photos/Getty Images; Mississippi Band of Choctaw Indians*; National Library of Medicine; MPI/Archive Photos/Getty Images; Capt. Travis Trueblood, U.S. Air Force*; Niall Carson/PA Images via Getty Images.

Cataloging-in-Publication Data
Names: Stewart, Mark, 1960 July 7-.
Title: Choctaw history and culture / Mark Stewart.
Description: Buffalo, NY : Cavendish Square Publishing, 2026. | Series: In focus: Native Americans | Includes glossary and index.
Identifiers: ISBN 9781502674739 (pbk.) | ISBN 9781502674746 (library bound) | ISBN 9781502674753 (ebook)
Subjects: LCSH: Choctaw Indians--Juvenile literature. | Choctaw Indians--Social life and customs--Juvenile literature.
Classification: LCC E99.C8 S94 2026 | DDC 976.004'97387--dc23

CPSIA compliance information: Batch #CS26CSQ: For further information contact Cavendish Square Publishing LLC at 1-877-980-4450.
Printed in the United States of America

CONTENTS

ABOUT OUR GLOSSARY

In this book, there may be several words or terms you are reading for the first time, or words that are familiar but used in an unusual way. All of these words appear in **bold type** throughout the book and are defined on page 30.

I AM THE LAND

The Mississippi River Valley is one of the most fertile agricultural areas in the world. The steady supply of food grown there has supported large numbers of humans for thousands of years. We know that large population centers existed because of the **ambitious** mound-building projects undertaken by the people who lived there. Most of the mounds in this region are around 2,000

This illustration from an early book shows two Choctaw women from the 1770s.

years old. Some in the Lower Mississippi Valley date back thousands of years before that. This is the area where the Choctaw people lived for many centuries.

The Nanih Waiya Mound in the state of Mississippi is central to the tribe's origin legend. It is unclear whether the mound-builders were direct ancestors of the Choctaws. However, the tribe has much in common with a great many of their **descendants** in the Southeast. Most

◀ The Mississippi River has supported multiple cultures over thousands of years.

experts believe that the tribe was formed in the 1500s from related groups that banded together around the time Europeans arrived. The number of Choctaws during this era was probably between 100,000 and 150,000.

The Choctaw people understood farming techniques that made the most of the landscape. They depended on corn, beans, and squash. Corn stalks provide a structure for beans, while squash grows on the ground. In combination, these plants deliver a **complete protein**. Knowledge of the environment also made the Choctaws expert hunters, trappers, and harvesters of fish

and shellfish. Choctaw tribal lands stretched across the states of Alabama, Louisiana, and Mississippi, and once encompassed between 35,000 and 40,000 square miles (90,700 and 103,600 sq km).

The Choctaws thrived as farmers and traders, enjoying peaceful relationships with their neighbors, including the Chickasaws, whose lands were located to the north. The languages spoken by the two tribes are very similar and are both part of the **Muskogean** group, which was spoken by Native people along the Mississippi River and east into Georgia and South Carolina.

◀ Stickball games have been an important part of Choctaw culture for centuries.

In recent years, evidence has emerged of human presence in North America much earlier than previously thought—perhaps as long as 30,000 years ago. The northern ice sheet would have been impenetrable at that time, meaning that these people would have arrived by sea. Were the Choctaws descendants of these early arrivals? Genetic research may one day provide an answer.

FIRST CONTACT

Beginning in the 1500s, European nations began casting a hungry eye toward North America, which offered abundant natural resources and open space that promised to increase their prestige and power at home. They called the Americas the "New World," ignoring the fact that Indigenous people like the Choctaws had been living there for thousands of years. Their thirst for land seemed unquenchable and was difficult for Native cultures to comprehend. In 1539, Spain sent Hernan de Soto to create a colony in North America and also search for gold.

De Soto arrived on Florida's west coast with hundreds of men. In 1540, he came into conflict with Tuskaloosa, a powerful chief whose territory included much of modern Alabama—and whose people were ancestors of the Choctaws. Spanish horses overwhelmed Tuskaloosa's warriors. Beginning in the 1600s, French and English settlers also arrived in the region. The Choctaws

Spanish horses and weapons overwhelmed Native Americans in the South.

enjoyed peaceful trading relationships with both. Because of their willingness to **interact** with their neighbors, the Choctaws were referred to as one of the "five civilized tribes." The other four were the Cherokees, Chickasaws, Seminoles, and Creek (Muscogee).

I AM A WARRIOR

Although Choctaw men of fighting age were **revered** as courageous hand-to-hand warriors, there was a very low level of conflict within their culture. Much of the fighting they did was related to their complex relationship with the European nations with whom they coexisted and traded. The Spanish colonized areas along the Gulf Coast, the English occupied land along the Atlantic Coast, and the French controlled the Mississippi on the western edge of Choctaw territory.

France and England were longtime enemies. This created bitter disagreement within the tribe over which side to favor as

◀ Peter Pitchlynn—also known as Snapping Turtle—was an important Choctaw military leader and diplomat.

Choctaw warriors helped a small American force defeat Great Britain at the Battle of New Orleans in 1815.

trading partners. This argument exploded into a **civil war** in 1747, with Choctaw killing Choctaw in a dispute that lasted three years. Deaths reached into the hundreds before the pro-French **faction** eventually won out.

In 1786, following the American Revolution, the Choctaws allied themselves with the United States. Most tribe members had sided with the colonists against the British. They adopted many American cultural and religious practices, hoping to become a part of the new nation. When the Shawnee chief Tecumseh asked the

Choctaws to join a Native rebellion against the U.S. in 1811, the most powerful Choctaw chief, Pushmataha, refused.

The Choctaw fought beside American soldiers during the War of 1812 against the British and their allies, including the Creeks, who were longtime enemies. More than 50 Choctaw warriors fought at the Battle of New Orleans in January 1815. Their ability to move silently around the **bayous** and strike the British from behind

played an important role in the outnumbered Americans' decisive victory.

The battle weapon of choice for the Choctaw was the war club. War clubs were usually made of hickory, a hardwood that is also somewhat flexible. Most had a ball-shaped head with a sharp projectile. Some had blades along the side, like European **broadswords**. Others were long and sharp at the top, similar to the lances favored by Spanish horsemen. The Choctaw fought in well-organized units and were quick to become experts with European axes and swords, as well as firearms.

The Choctaws' most admired tribal leader, Pushmataha, was a skilled warrior and diplomat. He traveled to Washington, D.C., in 1824 to demand that President James Monroe evict squatters from Choctaw territory. "No Choctaw ever drew his bow against the United States," he reminded the Secretary of War, John Calhoun. The raids that took Pushmataha to Arkansas and Oklahoma as a young man gave him important knowledge of these lands, which proved valuable in negotiating treaties with the U.S. government.

◀ A war club was a lethal weapon in the hands of a Choctaw fighter.

A NEW REALITY

Try as they might, the Choctaw people were unable to stem the tide of settlers in their lands. Hoping to live in peace with Americans, they exchanged their land for land west of the Mississippi River through a series of treaties. In 1830, the United States passed the Indian Removal Act, which claimed what little territory the Choctaws had left. The tribe was later forced to move to Indian Territory, in what would become the state of Oklahoma. Oklahoma is actually a Choctaw word, which combines the words for "people" (*okla*) and "red" (*humma*).

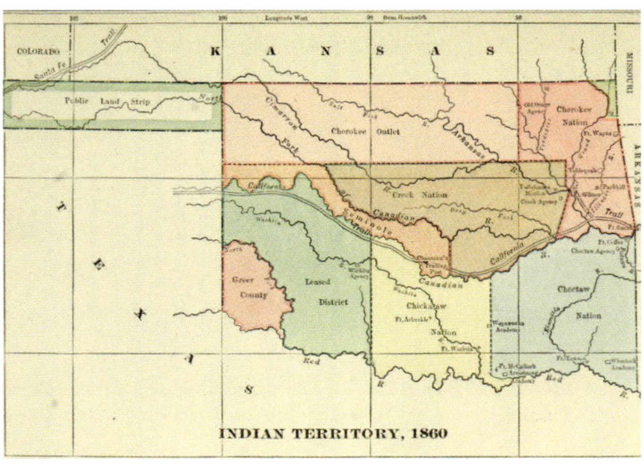

This 1860 map shows Choctaw territory in Oklahoma in light blue.

The Indian Removal Act of 1830 forced Choctaw families to move more than 500 miles (800 km).

The Choctaw people worked to rebuild their culture in their new home. However, in 1889, they found themselves in the path of American **expansion** once again. White settlers called homesteaders were given the opportunity to claim land in the Oklahoma Territory and came into conflict with the tribe. In 1907, Oklahoma became a state. Before it did, the government passed the Curtis Act, which forced the "five civilized tribes" to give up more than 90 million acres (36.4 million ha) that they had acquired in their treaties generations earlier.

BEING CHOCTAW

Before their forced relocation, the Choctaws lived in villages surrounded by fields that produced corn, beans, squash, and other food. Planting and tending to these crops typically was the responsibility of women and children. Knowledge of wild plants that could be harvested for food and medicine was passed down through the generations. Swamp cane, which was available in great abundance on Choctaw land, was used to make everything from baskets to bedding to dwellings. **Palmetto** leaves were also used in basket-making. Choctaw mothers carried their infants on cradleboards, which enabled them to do their work while keeping their children safe.

Women held positions of influence and power in Choctaw society and were celebrated as givers of life. Choctaw words for "love" and "holy"

This painting shows the Choctaw Eagle Dance. Spiritual celebrations have been important to the tribe's culture for centuries.

A Choctaw family moves through southern marshland. They often traveled barefoot during warm-weather months.

come from the word *hollo*, which refers to feminine power. Family relationships in Choctaw society were matrilineal, meaning they followed the women's ancestral line. During tribal functions, children sat on the mother's side of the fire, while fathers sat with their brothers and the children of their sisters.

Hunting and trapping was the responsibility of men. Choctaws relied on harvesting deer for meat, hide, and antlers. The wellbeing of a village was often linked to the size and health of the deer population in its environment. Choctaw hunters made great use of blowguns in killing birds and small game, such as squirrels and rabbits. The long, hollow tubes measured six feet or longer and demanded great patience and accuracy—and lots of practice. Choctaw hunters also used rabbit sticks, which looked like smaller versions of their war clubs, to take down their prey.

Choctaws revered their healers and spiritual leaders, believing they had the ability to move in and out of the spirit world. Prophets, who were called *hopaii*, guided people based on what the spirits told them. They possessed special powers, including the ability to influence the weather. Choctaw chiefs organized ceremonies and celebrations, the greatest being the Green Corn ceremony.

The Choctaws and their ancestors dressed lightly and usually traveled barefoot in all but the winter months. Men wore breechcloths that wrapped around the waist and between the legs, while women wore simple dresses. The trading relationship the Choctaws built with the French in the 1700s gave them access to cotton fabric,

and soon they adopted European-style clothing, including pants, shorts, and dresses.

When the Choctaws were forced to move west, they were able to maintain many of their traditions. For example, corn continued to play an important role—not just as a food source, but also in ceremonial life. The open space of their new home meant their hunting depended more on firearms. However, the blowgun still plays a role in ceremonies and competition. Indeed, both before and after the tribe's removal to Oklahoma, athletic contests played an important role in Choctaw society. Sports like *toli*—a stickball game similar to lacrosse—sometimes had hundreds of men and women playing, and many more gathered to watch.

▲ A Choctaw man poses with his toli stick.

Choctaw men were noted for the length of their hair compared to other tribes in the Southeast, who sometimes called them "Long Hairs." Often, they let a lock of hair grow extra-long over the right ear. This helped others identify them as Choctaw when they traveled.

◀ This painting shows how a Choctaw riverside camp might have looked in the early 1800s.

SOMETHING SACRED

The name Choctaw is believed to be related to a powerful chief named Chatah. European settlers began using this name in the 1600s, shortly after the tribe formed from groups of related people. However, Choctaw ancestors had lived in the region for thousands of years. Their most powerful creation myth holds that Nanih Waiya, the ancient platform mound in Eastern Mississippi, was the birthplace of all humankind.

According to legend, the Choctaws were the fourth and final tribe to emerge from Nanih Waiya. The Creeks were the first and headed east. They smoked

tobacco and set the woods on fire, erasing their path. Unable to follow, the Cherokees went north. The third tribe was the Chickasaws. They followed the Cherokees' trail north and settled near them. The Choctaws decided to stay near the sacred mound.

Choctaw beadwork often includes traditional themes.

Although the Choctaws embraced Christianity when they came into contact with European settlers, they also maintained several religious and cultural traditions. Their belief in supernatural beings dates back countless centuries. Nanapesa is a superior being that watched them through a "hole" in the sky (the sun). Because fire represented the sun, fire became important to the Choctaws beyond its use for cooking and

The Nanih Waiya mound in Mississippi is a central part of the Choctaw origin story.

heating. Ohoyo Osh Chishba introduced the Choctaws' ancestors to corn, while Kowi Anuk Asha were creatures that taught Choctaw doctors about medicine. Some supernatural beings captured, frightened, or harmed people. Nalusa Chito's place in tribal mythology has similarities with the devil.

After the tribe's removal to Oklahoma, swamp cane and palmetto leaves were no longer available for traditional basket-making. Many Choctaw artisans focused their creativity and attention on producing intricate beadwork, which they incorporated into jewelry

LeAnne Howe explores Native American themes in her books, plays, poetry, and films.

and ceremonial clothing. Choctaw beadwork became highly desirable outside the tribe among collectors and continues to evolve into new and exciting art forms.

The artistic tradition within the Choctaw culture extends to other fields, including literature. LeAnne Howe is a novelist, playwright, poet, and screenwriter. Her novel *Shell Shaker* won the American Book Award. Howe is a professor at the University of Georgia, where she teaches English and Creative Writing. Her writing and film work looks at different sides of the Native American experience. In the documentary *Indian Country Diaries: Spiral of Fire*, she traveled to North Carolina to show how the Cherokee tribe there has maintained its cultural traditions—and explored her own identity as the daughter of a Cherokee father she never knew.

Among the Choctaws' most important rituals is the Green Corn ceremony, a four-day festival celebrated by many tribes that once called the southeastern U.S. home. It occurs at the beginning of the annual harvest and involves feasting, fasting, and dancing.

PAST, PRESENT, FUTURE

Given how the Choctaw people were forcibly removed from their ancestral homeland—and stripped of their territory and rights by the United States government—it is remarkable how willingly and how well they have fought for their country. During World War I, American troops were at great risk after it was discovered that the enemy was able to break the codes they were using. Choctaw volunteers suggested using their language instead of English for secret communication, knowing that the Germans would be unable to **decipher** their words. These "code talkers" were recognized more than 70 years later by the French for helping to win the final battles of the war. During World War II, Choctaws provided

Young Choctaw children participate in a cultural event. This is one way the tribe preserves its traditions.

A group of Choctaw soldiers pose during World War I. The code talkers were recognized in a ceremony by the French in 1989.

the same service, as did the Navajos and other Native American soldiers.

Today, most Choctaws live in southeastern Oklahoma. The injustices they suffered there over more than a century finally started to be addressed by the work of **activists** in the final decades of the 1900s. In 1971, the Choctaw Nation of Oklahoma held its first election of a chief in more than 60 years. In 1983, the Choctaw people **ratified** a constitution that mirrored the U.S. Constitution. A Tribal Council was created to make laws, approve budgets, and make decisions about Choctaw property.

The Jena Band of Choctaws is located in central Louisiana. It has between 300 and 400 members.

In 2020, the **U.S. Supreme Court** rendered a decision on a court case (*McGirt v. Oklahoma*) that recognized more than a century of broken promises to the "five civilized tribes." As a result, the Choctaws gained more power and control over their lands in Oklahoma.

Some Choctaws never left the Southeast. They resisted removal in the 1830s—some by hiding, others by **passing** as white. More than a century later, the Mississippi Band of Choctaw Indians was finally recognized by the U.S. government. More than 11,000 people live on their reservation, which covers eight

Irish political leader Leo Varadkar poses with Choctaw tribe members in Oklahoma in 2018. The Choctaws sent money to Ireland during the potato famine of 1848–1852—forging a bond that is still strong today.

counties. In 2008, the band regained control over the Nanhi Waiya mound, their most sacred site. A third group, the Jena Band of Choctaw Indians, received federal recognition in 1995. Its reservation is located in central Louisiana.

For hundreds of years, the Choctaws have demonstrated a remarkable ability to absorb the cultural influences of the people with whom they come

into contact—and then make them their own. This quality has helped the tribe to succeed in a wide range of businesses, which employ thousands of people, and enabled Choctaw traditions to evolve and thrive. The tribe's commitment to providing education and health services to its people, and developing strategies to address everyday economic and social challenges, holds great promise for the future.

◀ Appearances by the Choctaw Nation Color Guard serve as a reminder of the tribe's contributions to the U.S. military.

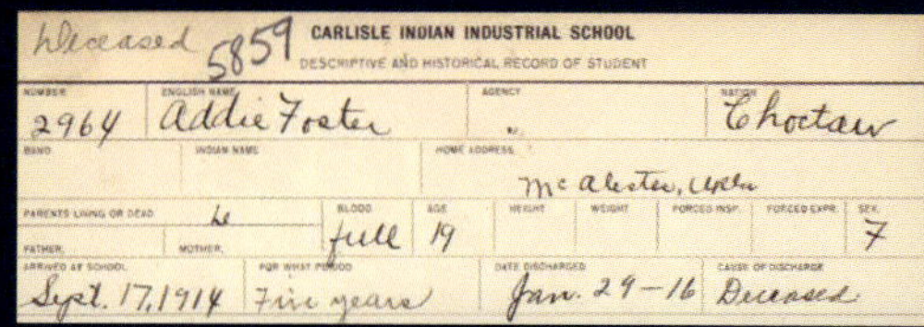

Choctaw children were among the thousands who were sent to government boarding schools, including the Carlisle Indian School in Pennsylvania. The goal of these schools was to **assimilate** young people into mainstream American society by teaching them skills and breaking tribal bonds. The experience was deeply traumatic for young Native Americans. This file for Addie Foster shows that she died less than two years after arriving at Carlisle.

GLOSSARY AND FURTHER READING

GLOSSARY

Activists—People who fight for social or political change.

Ambitious—Working toward a high level of success.

Assimilate—Become absorbed into a new culture.

Bayous—Marshy bodies of water.

Broadswords—Weapons made for slashing rather than thrusting.

Civil War—A conflict between citizens of the same nation.

Complete Protein—A protein that contains all nine amino acids the human body needs.

Decipher—Convert code into normal words or language.

Descendants—People related to those who came before them.

Expansion—The process of becoming larger or more extensive.

Faction—A group organized to oppose others within the same overall group.

Interact— Become directly involved with others.

Muskogean— A family of Indigenous languages originating in the Southeast.

Palmetto—A low-growing, fan-leafed palm tree.

Passing—A survival strategy sometimes used by people of color. "Passing" is complex and often controversial issue.

Ratified—Officially agreed to.

Revered—Deeply respected and admired.

U.S. Supreme Court—A group of judges responsible for interpreting the Constitution and resolving disputes that involve federal law as the final word on legal matters.

BOOKS

Krupat, Arnold. *Boarding School Voices: Carlisle Indian School Students Speak*. Lincoln, NE: University of Nebraska Press, 2021.

Rossiter, Brienna. *The Trail of Tears*. Mendota Heights, MN: North Star Editions, 2025.

Tyler, Ron. *Native Americans: The Complete Plates of McKenney, Catlin, and Bodmer*. Cologne, Germany: Taschen America, 2024.

Various Authors. *My Life: Growing Up Native in America*. New York, NY: MTV Books/Simon & Schuster Children's Publishing, 2024.

ABOUT THE AUTHOR

MARK STEWART has written more than 150 non-fiction books for educational publishers, covering history, sports, and popular culture. His family tree tells a complex story common to many Americans. Mark's ancestors include some of the first European colonists, as well as the Indigenous people with whom early settlers interacted. Some faced off on the field of battle while others fought side-by-side. His 10th great-grandfather was **Myles Standish**, an officer on the ***Mayflower***, while his ninth great-grandmother was **Singing Bird Corbison**, who was described as a "Shawnee woman" but who was probably from the **Wampanoag** tribe. The Wampanoag people saved Standish and his fellow **Pilgrims** from starvation during the winter of 1620–21, forming the basis for the story of Thanksgiving. The descendants of Corbison and Standish blended into a single family in 1789, and then headed west in search of opportunity. This brought Mark's ancestors into direct conflict with Native people along the frontier in the 1700s and 1800s. Mark's sixth great-grandmother recalled frantically casting bullets for her husband as they defended their small Kentucky fort from an attack. Another served under 23-year-old **Abraham Lincoln** in the Illinois Militia during the Black Hawk War of 1832. Mark's more recent ancestors chose to fight their battles with words—as writers and editors of books, newspapers, and magazines. In 2007, he authored a history of the **Indian Removal Act of 1830** and the infamous **Trail of Tears**.

INDEX